FAITH

actually

WORKS!

A Simple Manual

on the Principles of Faith

By Rev. Jean-Paul Engler

FAITH THAT ACTUALLY WORKS

ISBN-13: 978-1514622698

ISBN-10: 1514622696

Rev. Jean-Paul Engler
Jean-Paul Engler Ministries – FSCO
PO Box 423
NEW MARKET, TN 37820
www.fscoministries .org

Printed in the United States of America

CONTENTS

INTRODUCTION

As you might imagine, much consideration and prayer has preceded the writing of this book on faith. Volumes have already been written on the subject, by a number of authors much more knowledgeable and famous than I am.

While some may ask what can possibly be added to what so many have already taught on the subject, faith remains one of the least understood and scarcely applied principles in the Bible.

Since we've been called to live by faith, and know that without it it's impossible to please God, we obviously need to have a clear understanding on the matter.

The mechanics of faith should not be a mystery to the believer. God's intention is for us to become so proficient in this area that we spontaneously respond to any situation by faith, rather than with our human instincts.

I would like you to think of this book as a simple, uncomplicated, and to the point "instruction manual" on faith. Whether you're a veteran Christian with much experience in the area of faith or someone who's just begun their journey on the road to abundant life, you will be given step by step directions from Scripture on how to access all that God has made available to you by His grace.

If you're like me, instructions have to be simple, concise, and logical, if I am to successfully follow them. I promise you, you will not be confused by this book. Had I not feared to offend some readers, I initially considered calling it "Faith for Dummies"!

CHAPTER 1

LIVING BY FAITH

Consciously or not, we often regard faith as something to be used in extreme cases, or as a last resort, only after all other possibilities have been exhausted.

> *Your word is a lamp to my feet*
> *And a light to my path.*

Psalm 119:105

As Christians, we understand that God's Word should not be used occasionally, intermittently, or as a last ditch effort to get us out of a difficult situation. It should rather be used regularly and consistently. In the same way, faith needs to become as spontaneous to us as putting one foot in front of the other as we progress on our journey with Jesus.

> *For we walk by faith, not by sight.*

2 Corinthians 5:7

Walking by faith refers to a constant forward progression. We will do well to remember that walking, in the natural sense, didn't happen overnight. None of us walked out of the delivery room under our own power. There eventually came a time when we took our first steps under the applause of our loving parents. Although hesitant and awkward at first, walking eventually became as natural to us as breathing. And so it is with faith. The goal is to become so proficient in it that you no longer have to think about it. But don't think there won't be challenges on your way there.

CREATED TO WALK BY FAITH

The first key necessary to unlock the "mysteries" surrounding faith is to understand that God did not create man to rely solely on his natural eyesight or human perception to navigate through life.

When we study the story of creation, we discover that Adam and Eve initially "saw" through the eyes of God, their Creator!

Then God said, "Let Us make man in Our image, according to Our likeness;"

Genesis 1:26a

The Scriptures teach us that God's ways are not our ways and that He most definitely does not look at things the same way we humans do. While this is true, we need to understand that this distorted perception of things happened as a consequence of man's fall. Originally, Adam and Eve very much saw the way the Creator Himself saw. Listen to the words of Adam when he was first introduced to Eve:

"This is now bone of my bones
And flesh of my flesh;"

Genesis 2:23a

Obviously, Adam had no previous experience when it came to women. He had no reference of comparison, nor did he even know what a woman was supposed to look like. Without ever mentioning Eve's physical appearance or natural beauty, Adam strictly describes what God saw in the woman and the purpose for which He had created her. Adam saw her as one that came from him, came alongside him to help him and make him complete.

GOD'S PLAN SEVERLY ALTERED

Count on Satan to come and destroy God's perfect plan. What was the serpent talking about when he promised Eve that her eyes would be opened? Nothing suggests that Adam and Eve were physically blind. So what does Satan mean when he promises that their eyes would be opened?

What I believe the serpent is offering here is for Adam and Eve to choose an alternate way of seeing things, rather than continuing to rely on what God was revealing to them. This would of course mean that Satan could then influence their newly found perception of things.

The first thing they saw with their newly found eyesight was their nakedness. T.M.I., devil! This is information they could have done without! How could they not be aware of it? It's true that they weren't clothed in a physical sense, but clothed they were . . . with the glory of God! Unfortunately, they now had to depend on perishable leaves for clothing!

In II Corinthians 5:7 we previously quoted, the Apostle Paul makes a clear distinction between walking by faith rather than by sight. The sight he's referring to is the natural eyesight. Adam and Eve would have to rely on the sense of sight after disobeying their Creator. Their carnal eyesight thus became the primary way by which they would assess their surroundings and evaluate the means by which they would handle any situation. This was the equivalent of the default setting on your computer. It allowed

Adam and Eve to somehow continue to function on the earth, but with a much diminished capacity of perception and effectiveness. This switching from God's "eyesight" to the natural eyesight is perfectly illustrated by Adam's reference to Eve after the fall. She who used to be "bone of his bones and flesh of his flesh" has been demoted to:

The woman whom You gave to be with me

Genesis 3:12a

Would you agree that Adam no longer saw Eve as he saw her before? She went from being the perfect mate to becoming a convenient scapegoat!

WHAT IS FAITH, REALLY?

Nevertheless, when the Son of Man comes, will He really find faith on the earth?"

Luke 18:8b

I would like to draw your attention to the word "really" in this verse. What does Jesus mean by it?

He could probably have said it this way, "Will He find real faith on the earth?"

If there is such a thing as real faith, we have to assume that false faith also exists. Wishful thinking or presumptions are not expressions of faith. It is essential that we have a clear understanding of what faith really is.

Now faith is the substance of things hoped for, the evidence of things not seen.

Hebrews 11:1

When we search for a Bible definition of faith most of us immediately go to this verse. Just because we can quote it from memory doesn't mean we understand it, or that we're confident enough to apply it.

One can have a thorough understanding of the laws of aerodynamics, but proof of his confidence will only be revealed when he climbs into the airplane he just built and is actually willing to fly it!

As they say: this is where the rubber meets the road! I've met many people, including preachers, who have a great understanding of the "theory" of faith, but don't have the confidence to apply it to their own lives. I'll never forget this famous faith preacher who'd asked me to organize meetings for him in France. At first, I was very excited about the prospect of having so many people blessed by this ministry. But, as we came close to finalizing the details of the meetings, I discovered that the financial requirements made by this faith preacher were far beyond the realm of reason or of our possibilities. I have no doubt this man would have delivered convincing messages on the subject of faith. The problem was that I was no longer convinced that he practiced what he preached. It's one thing to know something, it's quite another to actually do it.

I like the way Jesus puts it:

If you know these things, blessed are you if you do them.

John 13:17

Since faith is such a fundamental part of our Christian lives, it is important that we fully understand it so we can put it to use with absolute confidence.

I will now attempt to explain faith, in a way even a child would be able to understand it.

WE WERE ALL GIVEN A MEASURE OF FAITH

You might be familiar with a scene in the first Indiana Jones movie where the hero skips from one stone to another hoping they won't give way as he lands on them.

If your faith walk resembles this hit and miss proposition, you really need a revelation of what faith really is.

When it comes to mechanics and do it yourself home improvements, the jury is still out on whether I'm qualified or not. But I do know this, while some projects require specialized tools for which one needs particular skills, others can be completed satisfactorily with basic tools found in just about every toolbox.

. . . as God has dealt to each one a measure of faith.

Romans 12:3

Think of the measure of faith you've been given as the "equipment" God has lovingly provided every man and woman to enable them to tackle any situation they will encounter in life.

When Jesus asked His disciples the question, "Where is your faith?" He wasn't implying that they had not been given the measure of faith allocated to every human being. Nor was He saying that some were cheated of the amount they deserved when He accused them of having "little faith." What we should understand is that in both cases those to whom Jesus addressed these words simply failed to use the measure of faith God had put at their disposal.

When we are told in Hebrews 11:6 that without faith it is impossible to please God, we must understand that this isn't talking about some unfortunate soul who was overlooked on the day faith was distributed. What it means is that we are displeasing God when we choose not to operate in the faith He has lovingly provided us.

A SIMPLE DEFINITION OF FAITH

In no way do I want to minimize the definition of faith expressed in Hebrews 11:1, but if you're like me you'll need instructions that don't require a PhD to figure out.

I've been known to return items to the store because the assembly instructions were too complicated or confusing. I am a great fan of K.I.S.S. Don't worry, I'm not talking about the rock band, but rather the "Keep It Simple, Stupid" principle.

The simplest definition of faith I can offer you is:

FAITH IS SEEING WITH THE EYES OF GOD.

I am reminded of a popular Christian song titled, "Her Father's eyes." This, of course, isn't referring to God's physical eyes, but rather to one's ability to see as the Father sees. In its simplest expression, this is what walking by faith is!

SEE YOUR ANSWER WITH YOUR EYES CLOSED

Almost every time I search for a misplaced item around our home, my wife invariably cautions me to look for the object with my eyes open! Following, is a story in the Bible where Jesus teaches us to do just the opposite in the realm of faith.

Jesus said to him, "Thomas, because you have seen Me, you have believed. Blessed are those who have not seen and yet have believed."

John 20:29

I personally know a few people to whom Jesus has appeared and who subsequently have given their lives to Him. But for most of us, we are among "those who have not seen and yet have believed," and for that reason Jesus calls us blessed!

This faith principle is certainly not limited to seeing Jesus, but it applies to all things we're believing God for.

FAITH IS NOW

Almost every translation of Hebrews 11:1 uses the words "Now faith is . . ." It wouldn't take much of a stretch to say that, "Faith is now."

We often perceive the realization of the miracle we're believing for as a future event. It is not! The very essence of faith is to receive now, in advance, and before it physically materializes; whatever we've asked the Lord to do for us!

Faith, in the realm of the Kingdom, is the equivalent of a certified check in the banking world. We may not be able to see and touch the actual currency appearing on the check, but it is proof that we indeed have it in our possession. Humanly speaking, we might prefer having the cold hard cash in our hands, but then faith would be completely unnecessary.

For we were saved in this hope , but hope that is seen is not hope; for why does one still hope for what he sees? But if we hope for what we do not see, we eagerly wait for it with perseverance.

Romans 8:24, 25

When we look at blessing, healing, or prosperity in the Bible we usually see it in the form of a promise. But God sees that blessing, healing, and prosperity as reality. For us, it is something we expect God to do. But for God, if it is contained in His Word, it is already done!

THE FAITH AND GRACE CONNECTION

The abundant life Jesus promises is provided through grace. The way by which divine grace is obtained is by faith. There is no other means by which to access what God has provided.

Salvation is a perfect example of this process. We understand that the grace needed for our salvation was provided long before we made the decision to ask Jesus into our hearts. Necessary provision was made before anyone even needed it.

. . . the Lamb slain from the foundation of the world.

Rev 13:8

The grace for our salvation was obviously provided through the redemptive work of Jesus. From that point on, all that was required was for us to receive the gift by faith as it was freely offered to us.

Think of it as a sizeable monetary deposit placed into your bank account by a benefactor. No matter the size of the deposit or how dramatically it could change your life, it will have absolutely no effect unless you actually make a withdrawal!

For by grace you have been saved through faith, and that not of yourselves; it is the gift of God, not of works, lest anyone should boast.

Ephesians 2:8, 9

When it comes to spiritual "withdrawals," the "measure of faith" we read about in Romans 12:3 is the equivalent of the access code your bank customarily provides you with. Just as this code allows you to withdraw what's in your account, faith gives you access to what God has made available to you by His grace.

WALKING AS JESUS WALKED

It is important to understand that Jesus fully functioned as a human during His time on earth. In other words, He didn't stack the deck in His favor because He was the Son of God. In fact, Jesus referred to Himself as "the Son of Man" more than forty times and only five times as the Son of God in the Gospel. I believe He was trying to make a point, don't you?

We need to reject the notion that Jesus is the only One qualified to access the resources, power and favor, God has made available to all His children.

Do you remember when Jesus needed to pay the temple tax for Himself and for Peter? He never bothered to check how much money was in the "ministry account." He immediately sent Peter to the lakeshore and ordered him to cast a line and pull out the first fish that came up. To Peter's surprise, the fish had in its mouth a coin of the exact monetary value that was needed to pay the tax!

Not for a moment, do I believe that this fish somehow materialized at the precise time that Jesus sent Peter on his mission. Nor do I believe that this coin was minted in heaven. There's no indication that there was anything special about this fish or the coin it carried.

This is a case of a common fish, dispatched to deliver a common coin, to meet a common need, in response to a request made by a common man that displayed an uncommon faith!

What lessons can we learn from this story?

1. Jesus **heard** from God that He was going to meet the need.
2. Jesus **saw** the fish, as well as the needed coin, with his spiritual eyes.

3. Jesus **acted** on what He saw and heard. He consequently received what the Father had already provided.

Whatever you need, or how urgently it needs to manifest, this principle will work every single time you apply it!

We find many other instances in the New Testament where Jesus demonstrates this faith principle:

One day, as Jesus was about to fulfill what had been prophesied by Zechariah, Jesus sent two of His disciples to a certain village. There, He told them, they would find the donkey that was to carry Him during his triumphal entry into Jerusalem. From His vantage point on the Mount of Olives there was absolutely no way for Jesus to see the donkey. Yet, He gave them the exact location and provided them with precise instructions on how to obtain it.

Once more, Jesus applied the three steps of the faith principle and obtained the transportation He needed.

And He sent out two of His disciples and said to them, "Go into the city, and a man will meet you carrying a pitcher of water; follow him. Wherever he goes in, say to the master of the house, 'The Teacher says, "Where is the guest room in which I may eat the Passover with My disciples?"' Then he will show you a large upper room, furnished and prepared; there make ready for us.

Mark 14:13-15

In all probability Jesus had never visited this particular house. Yet, He precisely located it, knew that it met His requirements, and was certain of the owner's willingness to let Him and His disciples use it. It's worth mentioning that this upper room did not mysteriously appear the moment Jesus sent His disciples out to secure it. It had been there all along, ready to be used for the purpose for which it was built.

WAIT FOR IT . . . WAIT FOR IT . . .

Let me share a wonderful testimony that illustrates what can happen when a pastor who has heard from God gets a vision of what's been promised him and patiently acts accordingly:

This search was several years in the process. I'm sure there were times during this process, that my friend experienced discouragement and frustration. Yet, he never doubted the promise God had made him. During a ten month period they had scoured every available property that met their criteria and put offers on three separate locations, all of which fell through. One day, my friend was approached by his realtor about a facility owned by his current landlord located immediately behind the existing church location. It was a 36,000 sq ft facility (3 times what they were looking for). Now here is the real miracle: when my friend began to look for a new location, not only wasn't this particular building for sale, but even if it had been, it would have been out of his financial range. But in God's timing, he was able to acquire it for less than 15% of it's original list price!

My friend **heard** from God, **saw** the promise with his spiritual eyes, and **acted** accordingly. He did this without ever doubting or wavering.

Allow me one last illustration from the ministry of Jesus:

Nathanael said to Him, "How do You know me?"

John 1:48a

It is obvious from this text that Jesus had never laid eyes on Nathanael until that day. From verse 46, we discover the possibility that Nathanael wasn't necessarily thrilled to meet this man from Nazareth! But listen to Jesus' disarming answer:

Jesus answered and said to him, "Before Philip called you, when you were under the fig tree, I saw you."

John 1:48b

Did you hear that? Jesus **saw** him under the fig tree, before his natural eyes were laid on him. Not only that, He was able to see that Nathanael was a true Israelite, in whom there was no deceit. Our spiritual eyes will cause us to see further and clearer than our natural eyes will ever be able to!

DELIVERED FROM A DEMON POSESSED CAR

Just in case you're still struggling with the idea that we can walk as Jesus did, allow me to share a personal testimony.

A few years ago, I owned a car that my wife and I used for our ministry in France. First, I want to say that this was not a car God had provided for me. I had bought this one on my own, simply because I wanted it. Faith had absolutely nothing to do with it. I soon found out that there would be consequences to my foolishness.

To this day, I'm still convinced that this car was demon possessed! There came a time when we would have to lay our hands on it, just to get it to start. Eventually, we had to lay hands on it and pray to get it to stop! Even when we removed the key from the ignition the engine would continue to run!

Things got progressively worse, to the point where I almost begged God to give me another vehicle. I was so desperate I was ready to accept any vehicle God would give me, as long as it had four wheels! On one occasion, I was driving down the winding road that would take me to Rouen. I was making yet another request to the Lord for whatever vehicle He could throw my way. Then, as I was coming around one of the many curves on this road, there it was, the beautiful, shiny, silver grey vehicle of my dreams! Only one problem . . . I was looking at a roadside billboard

Then I heard the Lord ask me this question, "Can you believe me for this car?"

In the natural, there was no possible way for me to purchase any car: especially not a new one! But because I had so clearly heard God's voice on the matter, it seemed as if all I could answer was, "Yes!"

You may not believe me, but this car on the billboard became mine, at the precise moment that I said, "Yes." I was so convinced of this that I told my wife that God had given us a brand new car the moment I returned home. I had to stop her from running outside to take a look at it, as she thought we already had it!

ABRAHAM, THE FATHER OF FAITH

We cannot close this chapter without mentioning Abraham, who is often referred to as the "Father of Faith." There is so much that we can learn from this man who maintained such a close relationship with God.

There are many episodes in this man's life that confirm that he legitimately earned that title. There's one episode that particularly stands out for me:

You'll recall the incident that led to the separation of Abraham from his nephew, Lot.

So Abram said to Lot, "Please let there be no strife between you and me, and between my herdsmen and your herdsmen; for we are brethren. Is not the whole land before you? Please separate from me. If you take the left, then I will go to the right; or, if you go to the right, then I will go to the left."

Genesis 13:8, 9

One might wonder if Abraham was suffering from failing eyesight when he made this offer to his nephew! Had he not noticed how well watered and beautiful the plain of Jordan was? Could he not rightfully exercise his elder's authority and claim the land?

This is the difference between someone who, like Lot, looks at things with the eyes of the flesh, and someone like Abraham who prefers to rely on the promises of God!

Lot's natural eyesight only allows him to see what can provide immediate gratification. Abraham, on the other hand, is able to see like God sees, beyond time and space, with the absolute assurance that it will come to pass.

WHAT YOU SEE, IS WHAT YOU GET

In a very real sense, only what you're able to see with your spiritual eyes can be yours.

"Lift your eyes now and look from the place where you are — northward, southward, eastward, and westward; for all the land which you see I give to you and your descendants forever."

Genesis 13:14, 15

God wasn't just asking Abraham to look at a piece of real estate that could potentially be his. But since he was receiving it by faith, Abraham could take immediate and effective possession of it.

On a much smaller scale, of course, I remember the day God gave us the property we currently live on. Based on our financial situation, there was absolutely no way for us to acquire it. However, as my wife and I walked back to the spot where our mailbox sits today, God unmistakably told us both that the property was ours. On that day, we effectively took possession of the property and eventually had the house built that we now live in.

See like God sees, beyond time and space, with the absolute assurance that it will come to pass.

CHAPTER 2

WHERE DOES FAITH COME FROM?

So then faith comes by hearing, and hearing by the word of God.

Romans 10:17

Since faith originates in the Word of God, and that hearing it properly determines the outcome, I thought it was worth consecrating an entire chapter on the importance of hearing.

To be able to receive all that God has promised us in His word, it is essential that we understand the following verse:

"Therefore take heed how you hear. For whoever has, to him more will be given; and whoever does not have, even what he seems to have will be taken from him."

Luke 8:18

We already learned the importance of developing our spiritual eyesight. Just as important, we need to grow in our ability to hear God with our spiritual ears. On several occasions during His earthly ministry Jesus said the following words, "If anyone has ears to hear, let him hear." It is obvious that He wasn't referring to physical ears. Listen to what the prophet Jeremiah had to say on the matter.

'Hear this now, O foolish people, Without understanding, Who have eyes and see not, And who have ears and hear not:'

Jeremiah 5:21

We absolutely need to reach a point in our walk with the Lord when we're able to clearly hear the voice of the Father while we read about a promise made to us in the Bible. Far too often we're satisfied with the logos (or letter) of the Word without pursuing further. Here is what the Apostle Paul had to say about this:

who also made us sufficient as ministers of the new covenant, not of the letter but of the Spirit; for the letter kills, but the Spirit gives life.

2 Corinthians 3:6

It is doubtful that we'll ever act decisively on any promise that was merely heard with our natural ears or read with our natural eyes only. When one receives a Rhema word from the Father concerning their healing, deliverance, or blessing, they will assuredly become a doer of that word and not a hearer only!

"Therefore whoever hears these sayings of Mine, and does them, I will liken him to a wise man who built his house on the rock:"

Matthew 7:24

I'm sure that you've witnessed people who've just been prayed for, but their demeanor and their words continue to express defeat. You can be sure that they don't have a revelation of what they received. You can, therefore, conclude that they're not walking by faith, at least not in that particular instance.

I believe this is exactly what James was saying when he famously wrote: "faith without works is dead" (James 2:26). Faith requires action. If we refuse, or are unwilling to act on what the Word of God tells us, it is proof positive that we haven't heard with our spiritual ears and we don't have a revelation on the matter.

IT ALL ORIGINATES WITH GOD'S WORD

Referring back to Romans 10:17 which I previously quoted, we need to realize that the Word of God constitutes the very foundation of faith. Think of what you're needing the Lord to do for you, in terms of a building you're attempting to erect. Unless you have a scriptural basis for your request, your "house" has no foundation.

"In the beginning was the Word, and the Word was with God, and the Word was God. He was in the beginning with God. All things were made through Him, and without Him nothing was made that was made."

John 1:1-3

When it comes to faith, you can also think of the Word of God as the raw material necessary as the very basis of the faith process.

Once we have God's word on a subject, (and I don't just mean a Bible verse taken out of context), there's absolutely nothing that can keep us from receiving a promise made to us. The only thing that can possibly stand in the way is our own doubt and unbelief.

Heaven and earth will pass away, but My words will by no means pass away.

Mark 13:31

To further stress the importance of having a word from God before we can launch out on a faith journey, let's look at two Scriptures that illustrate how fundamental this is: One can be found in the Old Testament:

Unless the LORD builds the house, They labor in vain who build it;

Psalm 127:1a

The other is located in the New Testament:

"Therefore whoever hears these sayings of Mine, and does them, I will liken him to a wise man who built his house on the rock: and the rain descended, the floods came, and the winds blew and beat on that house; and it did not fall, for it was founded on the rock."

Matthew 7:24, 25

Nothing can shake the confidence of someone who has clearly heard from the Lord on a subject. Once we have reached that level of certainty, we can act on what we've heard with unshakable confidence. Abram changed his name from Abram to Abraham after God told him that he'd be a "father to many nations" (Genesis 17:4). We too will be able to make quality decisions based on the absolute assurance that we've heard from God on a particular matter.

When Jesus considered what the world's spiritual condition would be upon His return, He knew that there would be false teachers who'd minimize, edit, modify, corrupt, and compromise the Word of God.

Thus you have made the commandment of God of no effect by your tradition.

Matthew 15:6b

The diluting of the Word of God is, of course, nothing new. Jesus had to deal with this issue during His earthly ministry. What is new, however, is the increasing number of people with itching ears that are willing to listen to what the Bible calls fables. False teachers today have found a captive audience of men and women who are more interested in the popularity and charisma of the preacher than the scriptural validity of their message (2 Tim 4:3, 4).

". . . receiving the engrafted word, that is able to save your souls;"

James 1:21

(YLT)

Obviously, the Word has to first be received before it can be sown into our lives and circumstances. If we're the type of Christian that rarely, if ever, opens their Bible, or listens to the Word being preached, chances of a harvest are slim to none!

If we are to experience a victorious life of faith, we'll not only need to develop a serious appreciation for the Word of God, but also grow in our relationship with Jesus . . . the Word that was made flesh.

As we grow closer to the Shepherd and become more and more like sheep capable of hearing His voice, our level of trust and confidence will increase considerably.

WILL YOU GET ON HIS BACK?

If we are to walk by faith on a consistent basis, our trust in God's willingness and ability to do what He's promised in His Word is of the utmost importance.

Because all of creation testifies of His power, most of us are convinced of God's ability to perform whatever He says He can. Then, there is the question of whether He's willing to do it. Assuming that we can also answer this in the affirmative, we're now faced with the trust issue.

Allow me to illustrate with the true story of a fellow Frenchman by the name of Jean-Francois Gravelet, who stunned the world on June 30, 1859, as he walked across Niagara Falls on a tightrope. After successfully making the crossing, he asked the audience whether they believed that he could do it again. Since the crowd had seen him do it the first time with apparent ease, they shouted out, "Yes you can!" As he was making preparation to cross the falls for a second time, and because everyone seemed so confident in his ability to perform, he asked for a volunteer to climb on his back. Surprisingly, not a single person volunteered!

We may be absolutely convinced of God's ability and willingness to move on our behalf, but until we achieve an extreme level of trust through our personal relationship with Him and faith experiences, it's doubtful that we'll "climb on his back"!

USE YOU OWN FAITH

As true faith has become a rare commodity in this modern age, more and more Christians have come to rely more and more on other people's faith.

"When Jesus saw their faith, He said to the paralytic, "Son, your sins are forgiven you."

Mark 2:5

To be sure, Jesus saw the faith of the men carrying the paralytic's bed. But let's not overlook the faith of the one laying on the bed! I am convinced that his faith was every bit as strong as that of his friends who brought him to Jesus!

Time after time, Jesus would tell the men and women He had just healed: *"your faith has made you whole".*

The story of the man at the Pool of Bethesda, is very telling. This poor man had suffered from his infirmity for thirty eight years. Jesus came to him, asking his a very simple question: "Do you want to be made well?'

You would think that after all these years of suffering, this man would jump at the opportunity offered to him and shout YES! But this would have required faith on his part. His answer demonstrates his inability to see past his natural limitations.

"Sir, I have no man to put me into the pool when the water is stirred up; but while I am coming, another steps down before me."

John 5:7

Once, when the disciples were caught in a violent storm and they feared for their lives, Jesus again asked them the famous question: "where is your faith?".

Obviously, Jesus' faith was never an issue. He was simply wondering where their faith was! When Jesus said *"let us go to the other side"*, he never doubted for a moment that they would. In fact, he was so confident that he would have slept through the whole ordeal, had the disciples not woken him!

The disciple's problem could be summarized in this: they only heard the words of Jesus through their physical ears. Far too often, people will listen to a message or read a bible verse, treating it as they were the words spoken by a man. The disciples failed to understand that the words of Jesus were Spirit and life and thus heaven, earth, storms or obstacles, would have to yield to them!

CHAPTER 3

FAITH WITHOUT WORKS IS DEAD

Thus also faith by itself, if it does not have works, is dead But someone will say, "You have faith, and I have works." Show me your faith without your works, and I will show you my faith by my works. You believe that there is one God. You do well. Even the demons believe — and tremble! But do you want to know, O foolish man, that faith without works is dead?

James 2:17-20

You don't have to be a spiritual giant to understand that works – or corresponding action are necessary to complete the process of faith.

Imagine that a salesman offers you a product you absolutely cannot do without. You've heard everything that this item can do to bless your life. You have even expressed your approval as the salesman made his presentation. The salesman now presents you with a contract he expects you to sign. He's sure of the quality of his product and is convinced that you need it. But unless you take action and sign the purchase order you will not enjoy the benefits of the product. For all practical purposes the deal is "dead," because there were no "works" to validate the transaction.

THE SECRET OF THE SEED SOWN

As Jesus was explaining this particular parable of sowing to His disciples, He went out of His way to point out its spiritual significance.

And He said to them, "Do you not understand this parable?
How then will you understand all the parables?"

Mark 4:13

What Jesus is conveying to His disciples is that this particular parable holds the key that unlocks the mysteries contained in every other parable.

Let's see if we can unlock this "mystery" parable together:

"The sower sows the word."

Mark 4:14

First, we want to establish that God is the one who does the sowing of the Word. His reputation is flawless and He can absolutely be trusted. We must absolutely settle the issue of trust before we can proceed in our quest. Think of it as the first digit on the tumbler of an imaginary safe. For some of us, because we've been betrayed by men in our past, this could be a difficult hurdle to overcome. But overcome it we must!

Second, we need to settle in our heart that the Word (seed) is good. Because God is good, His Word cannot be anything else but good. If the Word does not produce the anticipated results, we cannot blame God (the sower), nor the Word (the seed). The answer must obviously lie elsewhere.

Even the most inexperienced fisherman knows that if there are no fish on the left side of the boat, there's absolutely no reason for there to be any on the right side!"

Even if somewhat reluctantly, Peter obeys what he perceives to be a command, rather than a suggestion. What follows is one of the most amazing fish story in the entire Bible! I suspect that Peter's obedience had a lot to do with his walking on water experience, as he walked out of the boat at Jesus' command.

While I'm somewhat suspicious of people who routinely challenge established laws of physics or general standards, we must understand that God is not limited by the laws He's put in place.

Logical thinking and basic fishing standards might be excellent guidelines to follow, but when they stand in the way of God Almighty who's given us permission to ignore them, like Peter, we must obey.

Is this not written in the Book of Jasher? So the sun stood still in the midst of heaven, and did not hasten to go down for about a whole day.

Joshua 10:13

By all accounts, Joshua wasn't a dreamer who went out of his way to violate God's natural laws. But when it became necessary for time to stand still in order for him to defeat the Amorites, Joshua didn't hesitate to order for the sun and moon to halt their course in the heavens!

The limitations that God has imposed on man, are very real. But those limitations don't apply to God or His ability to intervene on our behalf.

You might encounter situations in your life, where common sense and logic simply won't suffice. Those are times you'll need to remember that things that are very much impossible with men, are totally possible with God! Who knows? Maybe you too will see God perform a miracle that defies the laws of physics, like He did for Joshua!

BLIND BARTIMAEUS

If I had to choose among all the New Testament characters, there's one that particularly stands out to me, when it comes to faith.

That man would be the one usually called "blind Bartimaeus". We don't know exactly how long Bartimaeus had suffered from blindness before he received his healing miracle. What we do know, is that his condition was not a new development. It appears that he had occupied his begging spot along the road for quite some time.

But from the very moment that he heard that Jesus was walking nearby, he put his faith in action. Notice that he didn't request anyone to help him approach Jesus? In fact, not only did he totally ignore those who asked him to be quiet, but he shouted even louder to get Jesus' attention!

To me, verse 50 is particularly significant:

"And throwing aside his garment, he rose and came to Jesus"

Mark 10:50

Throwing aside a garment may not mean very much nowadays. But back then and under those circumstances, this was a defining moment in the life of Bartimaeus:

1. The garment he wore, was specifically worn by beggars. It was of a particular design and a uniform of sorts.

2. Disposing of it as he did, meant that he no intention of ever returning to his begging "profession".

3. It also meant that he never doubted that Jesus would heal him of his blindness

4. Spiritually, it also signifies that Bartimaeus didn't allow what represented his past, to affect his future.

We should all learn for Bartimaeus' example of faith. He may have been physically blind!... But his spiritual eyes were wide open!

JESUS HAS A CONVERSATION WITH A TREE

On one occasion, Jesus and His disciples were walking toward the city of Bethany. As they approached, Jesus saw a fig tree from which He expected to gather fruit. But, noticing that the tree was barren, he proceeded to curse it. When He returned the next day, His disciples expressed how surprised they were at seeing that the tree had actually withered. Listen to Jesus' response:

"Assuredly, I say to you, if you have faith and do not doubt, you will not only do what was done to the fig tree , but also if you say to this mountain, 'Be removed and be cast into the sea,' it will be done. And whatever things you ask in prayer, believing, you will receive."

Matthew 21:21-22

When Jesus spoke to the tree, He never had any doubt about the outcome. He didn't sneak out in the cover of night, to check on the progress of His curse. He simply didn't doubt.

Regardless of what we're believing for, doubt should never be allowed to penetrate. Faith and doubt cannot mix. Whichever we allow to rule, will determine whether we receive what we've asked for from the Lord.

"But let him ask in faith, with no doubting, for he who doubts is like a wave of the sea driven and tossed by the wind. For let not that man suppose that he will receive anything from the Lord; he is a double-minded man, unstable in all his ways."

James 1:6-8

It is, of course important for us to believe that God can accomplish whatever it is we're believing Him for. Believing that He actually wants to do it, is another step in the right direction, But knowing, beyond a shadow of a doubt that He has already done it for us, is what real faith is all about!

For those of you with methodical minds, we can present the process that the seed (word) has to go through in the following way:

1. **God is the only One who can sow the original seed. (Word)**

2. **The seed then needs to take root in the recipient's heart.**
   (Soil condition)

3. **Finally, the seed must be sown into our own circumstances by taking corresponding action. (Work)**

While it's true that the Lord watches over His word to perform it, this does not mean that He will do it in spite of us, against our will, or without our participation.

THE GREAT DECEPTION

When Jesus wondered whether He would *"really find faith on the earth"* in Luke 18:8, I'm certain that He was aware of the deceptive teachings that would run rampant in the last days.

What some modern preachers are suggesting today is that since God is love, everyone will automatically benefit from His grace, regardless of their heart condition or the level of their faith.

According to this teaching, the soil (heart) condition in this key parable is totally irrelevant. But Jesus is very clear when He declares that only the seed that fell on good ground yielded the anticipated harvest.

SEEDTIME, AND HARVEST

There are laws and principles that God has established that will never change, no matter how much some may want to fight against them or attempt to change them.

We may not like the natural law of gravity, but we understand that if we ignore it there may be disastrous consequences.

The same is true about spiritual laws. They may appear to be constraining to someone who's been caught up in today's humanistic philosophy. To be clear, anyone who's motto is, "If it feels good, just do it," will have difficulty submitting to laws God has put in place for all eternity.

"While the earth remains, seedtime and harvest , Cold and heat, Winter and summer, And day and night Shall not cease."

Genesis 8:22

In the natural world the seed is the initial element in the harvest process. To put it simply, no seed = no harvest!

We know from God's Word all that the Kingdom has to offer and all that God wants to make available to us, presents itself in the form of a seed.

"To what shall we liken the kingdom of God? Or with what parable shall we picture it? It is like a mustard seed which, when it is sown on the ground, is smaller than all the seeds on earth; but when it is sown, it grows up and becomes greater than all herbs, and shoots out large branches, so that the birds of the air may nest under its shade."

Mark 4:30-32

We obviously want everything God and His kingdom can provide for us. Unfortunately, nothing will happen unless the seed is first received, and then sown in whatever area we're seeking a harvest.

DON'T EAT YOUR SEED . . . SOW IT!!

As a believer, you know that God desires to supply all of your needs in the area of finances. Unfortunately, many Christians continue to be frustrated because they do not experience the promised blessing.

Now may He who supplies seed to the sower, and bread for food, supply and multiply the seed you have sown . . .

2 Corinthians 9:10

Beyond the tithe, which belongs to God, the Lord makes a clear distinction between the seed He entrusts us with for a future harvest, and the bread He gives us to meet our daily needs.

If we fail to sow our finances into whatever field the Lord directs us to do it in, we're ignoring the spiritual law God has put in place. Again, this may go against what our flesh, our logic, or what our accountant may have to say about it. Nevertheless, just as the natural law of gravity continues to be in effect, the law of seed, time, and harvest will prevail as long as the earth remains!

LORD, ARE YOU SURE ABOUT THIS?

There have been a number of occasions when the Lord prompted us to sow while it made no sense whatsoever!

On one such occasion, my wife Josette and I were walking back to our car after a meeting in Denver. Suddenly, my wife stopped in her tracks and asked if she could give some money to the homeless man we'd just passed. There wouldn't be anything unusual about this except that this money was all we had in our possession. In fact, we had to pray for a miracle of multiplication of gasoline just to make it back home! To our surprise, when we tried to see where the man had gone after receiving the money, he was nowhere to be found. We concluded that it must have been an angel!

I think this would have been a cool experience even if it had ended there, but it didn't. Not long afterwards, my wife had to make another important trip to Denver. Not that it was the first time this ever happened, but there was no money to put gas in the car. From where we lived, it was over 100 miles to her destination, and then, of course, she would have to come back. This was when the miracle happened: Not only did she make the mostly downhill trip to her appointment, but she was able to make the uphill return trip, all the way to our local gas station, where I met her to fill the tank!

We're both convinced that sowing into the angel/homeless man's life a few weeks earlier made it possible for this miracle to happen!

When Jesus told His disciples that they were "of little faith," we know that He was in no way implying that they had been cheated out of the measure of faith that the Father has bestowed on all mankind. What He was referring to was their unwillingness or inability to use the measure of faith they had at their disposal.

And the apostles said to the Lord, "Increase our faith."

Luke 17:5

This truth becomes even more evident as we study Jesus' response to the apostles' request.

"If you have faith as a mustard seed, you can say to this mulberry tree, 'Be pulled up by the roots and be planted in the sea,' and it would obey you."

Luke 17:6

Had Jesus forgotten the disciples' question? No, but He's directing them back to the fundamental seed principle He had taught them through the Mark 4:14 parable.

No matter how little experience you have in the area of faith, I encourage you to use the measure of faith you have been given. God does not expect you to tackle a "Goliath" on yourfirst outing, but He does expect you to be faithful with what you have been given.

Your first "lion" may be as benign as a head cold. But once you defeat it by the power of God, it will serve as a reference of victory if you ever have to face a "bear" or a "Goliath" in the future.

SEE YOURSELF WITH THE EYES OF FAITH

I hope that by now I've convinced you that we must learn to see with the eyes of the Spirit if we want to truly walk by faith.

The main reason many Christians never seem to receive anything from the Lord is because they have chosen to look at everything, including themselves, with the eyes of the flesh.

Therefore, from now on, we regard no one according to the flesh. Even though we have known Christ according to the flesh, yet now we know Him thus no longer. Therefore, if anyone is in Christ, he is a new creation; old things have passed away; behold, all things have become new.

2 Corinthians 5:16, 17

Sometimes we're just too quick in reading some Scriptures; thus, missing some extremely vital elements. When Paul tells us that he will no longer regard anyone according to the flesh, we have a tendency to forget that we're included on the list.

It will be extremely difficult, if not impossible, for anyone to walk by faith if he or she still sees themselves through the eyes of the flesh. If Jesus is indeed the Lord of our lives we have effectively become "new creations."

Contrary to Scripture, the way we perceive ourselves is often in a way that resembles who we used to be before Christ.

Reconcile the perception you have of yourself with what the Scriptures say you've become in Christ.

WHO DO YOU THINK YOU ARE?

One of the main characteristics of faith is that it gives us access to things that lie beyond the realm of human possibilities. This is best described by Jesus when He tells His disciples, "What things are impossible with men, are possible with God" (Matthew 19:26).

When God shared His plan to liberate Israel from the hands of the Egyptians, Moses was overwhelmed that he would even be considered to play a part in this grandiose event.

Understandably, anyone would have been intimidated by such a huge responsibility. But for Moses, the challenge was even greater, due to his tumultuous past. After all, wasn't he a fugitive who had killed a man and who's picture appeared in every Post Office in Egypt?

When Moses realized that God had chosen him to lead the people out of bondage, the words out of his mouth expressed the perception he had of himself:

"Who am I that I should go to Pharaoh, and that I should bring the children of Israel out of Egypt?"

Exodus 3:11

Much can be learned from Moses' response. Who does Moses think he is at this particular moment? Not only is he hiding from the law, but all he had been doing for the past 40 years was tending his father-in-law's sheep. Let's face it; not a single person on earth is truly capable of doing what God has purposed to accomplish through a human being.

For as he thinks in his heart, so is he.

Proverbs 23:7a

CHAPTER 4

IS IT FAITH, OR IS IT PRESUMPTION?

I fondly remember watching one of my favorite preachers, Pastor Wayne Myers, illustrate his teaching on presumption by using a comb. He would always carry a comb in his back pocket. Observing the scarcity of hair on his head, one would immediately wonder, "What could possibly be the purpose of the grooming tool in his pocket?" Things would become very clear once he would run the comb over his bald head. It would become even more obvious when he asked the following question, "Is this faith, or is it presumption?"

The audience would obviously have a big laugh over the illustration, but all would perfectly understand the message he was trying to convey.

In the previous chapter we spoke about the necessity of having God's Word on a petition we're expecting the Lord to fulfill. Before that, we learned that faith is seeing what already is, through the eyes of God.

A number of years ago, I had been very troubled by the teaching of a well-known preacher on the subject of faith. He was encouraging his audience to imagine whatever it was they were believing God for, suggesting that if they did it long enough and with enough passion, it would be granted to them.

This kind of teaching can be quite confusing for some. On one hand, we understand that receiving a rhema word from the Lord is the very foundation of the faith process. But Jesus told His disciples that they could have anything they asked for in prayer as long as they believed!

"And whatever things you ask in prayer, believing, you will receive."

Matthew 21:22

Was Jesus mistaken when He taught this? Certainly not! If one understands the teaching of the parable of the sower, as we previously studied, there is no possible confusion. Whatever things we ask for in prayer, we can believe we have received them because we have already seen them with the eyes of faith.

Back to the topic of imagining something we want until it somehow materializes. Let me be perfectly clear about this: it has absolutely nothing to do with faith! In fact, it is diametrically opposed to the Word of God:

Casting down imaginations, and every high thing that exalteth itself against the knowledge of God, and bringing into captivity every thought to the obedience of Christ;

2 Corinthians 10:5   KJV

Is it any wonder why so many Christians are frustrated because their prayers remain unanswered? Real faith always produces real results. Vain imaginations will only cause you to doubt God; thus, keep you from receiving anything from the Lord (James 1:6).

FAITH IS EVIDENT

From the text in Hebrews 11:1 we learned that, "faith is the evidence of things not seen." By now, you understand that just because things cannot be seen with the natural eye doesn't mean they can't be seen with the eyes of the Spirit.

In this definition of faith we find two words often used in the judicial realm: **substance** and **evidence**. Sometimes these two words are combined to form substantial evidence.

Faith should never be mistaken for wishful thinking or vain imaginations. Jesus considered the coin He saw in the mouth of the fish to be hard evidence. To Him, this was a much more reliable provision than whatever money could be found in the ministry purse carried by Judas!

DOUBT & UNBELIEF

Doubt and unbelief are close relatives! Whenever you find doubt, you can be sure of one thing: the absence of faith. The same is true for unbelief. You may recall that Jesus Himself couldn't do any mighty works in His hometown of Nazareth because of their unbelief.

Unbelief and doubt are to faith what kryptonite is to Superman! When Jesus perceived unbelief in the group of relatives surrounding a dead girl He'd been asked to pray for, He had to clear the room before He could proceed with the resurrection.

But let him ask in faith, with no doubting, for he who doubts is like a wave of the sea driven and tossed by the wind. For let not that man suppose that he will receive anything from the Lord; he is a double-minded man, unstable in all his ways.

James 1:6-8

I am confident that most believers I've ever prayed for have made their petition to the Lord in faith. Far too often, though, if their miracle didn't come immediately, doubt would creep in and their prayer remained unanswered.

Was it because they didn't ask in faith? Or was it because Jesus didn't want to bless them? You and I know the latter isn't true. What happened is exactly what happened to those Jesus mentioned in Mark 4:16, 17. They received God's promise with gladness, but when the promise was challenged by an apparent testing of their faith, doubt eventually won out.

THE HIGH COST OF PRESUMPTION

The rewards of operating in faith are obviously tremendous. However, we sometimes forget that being presumptuous has dire consequences.

Then the LORD spoke to Moses, saying, "Take the rod; you and your brother Aaron gather the congregation together. Speak to the rock before their eyes, and it will yield its water; thus you shall bring water for them out of the rock, and give drink to the congregation and their animals."

Numbers 20:7, 8

I'm sure that Moses would never have taken the liberty of striking the rock had he anticipated that it would keep him from entering the Promised Land.

God had instructed him to strike the rock on a previous occasion. Why couldn't he do it again in the same way? Because God is not limited, nor is He obligated to do things in the same manner every time. Jesus, whom we know to be "the same yesterday, today and forever" (Hebrews 13:8) did not heal blind folks in the same way every time!

When it comes to faith, there's one very important lesson we must learn: let God be God and do not ever try to put Him in a box!

Human beings are creatures of habit. We like for our proverbial "ducks" to be all neatly lined up and hate for anything or anyone to disturb our "perfect" order.

Allow me to say that the more this scenario fits you, the more difficult it will be for you to embrace the faith walk. It's not so much that the Lord wants to keep you wondering about His next move, but He does want you to rely on Him every minute and every second of every day!

THE PROBLEM WITH PRIOR EXPERIENCE

I love to hear testimonies about people who have experienced a miracle in their lives. Whether a financial or a physical healing, it is a great boost to our faith.

Unfortunately, the way by which God chose to respond in a particular instance often becomes the reference we hijack for our own purpose.

King Saul was no rookie when it came to military experience. Since his heart was not with the Lord, he could only count on himself, or rely on his army and weapons to fight any of his battles. He sincerely wanted to help David when he offered him his sword and armor:

So Saul clothed David with his armor, and he put a bronze helmet on his head; he also clothed him with a coat of mail. David fastened his sword to his armor and tried to walk, for he had not tested them. And David said to Saul, "I cannot walk with these, for I have not tested them." So David took them off.

1 Samuel 17:38, 39

"I went out after it and struck it, and delivered the lamb from its mouth; and when it arose against me, I caught it by its beard, and struck and killed it. Your servant has killed both lion and bear; and this uncircumcised Philistine will be like one of them . . ."

1 Samuel 17:35, 36

David's experience with the lion and the bear teaches us a very valuable lesson:

What David chose to remember from his experience with the lion and the bear is that it was God who delivered them into his hand. He even remembers the method he used to subdue the animals, catching them by their beards. But in no way does his previous experience limit him as he faces his new challenge.

What good are your previous successful experiences if your "Goliath" doesn't have a beard that can be pulled? How helpful is someone else's experience with an armor and sword when you have no idea how to use them?

Like David, you're much better off trusting God to show you the method and provide you with the weapons you need to win the battle you're facing.

BEWARE OF RELIGIOUS BLINDNESS

Jesus described the religious leaders of His time as "blind leaders." Of course, we know that He wasn't referring to a physical impairment, but rather to a spiritual condition.

> *"They are blind leaders of the blind. And if the blind leads the blind, both will fall into a ditch."*
>
> Matthew 15:14c

How did those who were supposed to successfully lead others on their spiritual journey become blind? I am sure that many things contributed to their demise. I believe the most important one is that they valued their position and their religious identity more than their love for God.

I wish this problem could have disappeared with the passing of the Pharisees. Alas, it has not! Today we're just as vulnerable to that spirit as the scribes, doctors of the law, and Pharisees were in those days.

So severe was their spiritual blindness (i.e., lack of faith) that they were incapable of seeing Jesus as the very Messiah they were eagerly waiting for.

Every time we're confronted with something unfamiliar, do we immediately reject it? Do we try to make it fit our denominational or religious framework by referencing what we've been taught, or our own limited experience; rather than the Word of God?

If this description fits you, you're in danger of being in the same situation as the Laodicean Church, as recorded in Revelation 3:17. That church was obviously blind, but had not awareness of it.

If you want your spiritual eyes to be opened, I urge you to do what Jesus recommended:

"anoint your eyes with eye salve, that you may see."

Revelation 3:18c

CHAPTER 5

THE POWER OF YOUR WORDS

According to Hebrews 4:12, we know that the Word of God is extremely powerful. What we often forget is what comes out of our mouths, positive or negative, has a powerful effect on our lives and circumstances.

Death and life are in the power of the tongue,

Proverbs 18:21a

The Bible has much to say about the tongue. We get the most valuable description of its power in the Epistle of James.

My brethren, let not many of you become teachers, knowing that we shall receive a stricter judgment. For we all stumble in many things. If anyone does not stumble in word, he is a perfect man, able also to bridle the whole body.

James 3:1

1. The first lesson we learn from this passage of Scriptures is to keep the use of our tongue to a minimum. This is not only true in the spiritual realm, but also in everyday life. How many divorces could have been avoided, and jobs preserved if someone would have just kept quiet.

Indeed, we put bits in horses' mouths that they may obey us, and we turn their whole body.

James 3:3

1. From this verse we learn that if one develops the ability of controlling his tongue, his entire life will be kept in check.

Look also at ships: although they are so large and are driven by fierce winds, they are turned by a very small rudder wherever the pilot desires.

James 3:4

2. What a powerful illustration of the power of the tongue! Proportionally, the rudder of a ship is a very small part of the structure. Yet, it is able to turn a vessel in whatever direction the captain wants it to go. It is comforting to know that this can be accomplished in spite of fierce winds. Let's make sure we remember this next time we find ourselves in an adverse situation. If life circumstances push us in a direction we know to be contrary to God's Word, only our tongue is what will change the course of events.

3. Jesus didn't beg, cry, or even pray to the Father when He found Himself in the storm. He used His tongue. End of story!

Even so the tongue is a little member and boasts great things. See how great a forest a little fire kindles!

James 3:5

4. In spite of its relatively small size the tongue is one of the most powerful members of the body. It can set in motion a course of events no one could have anticipated. One command, delivered by the proper authority, can dispatch an entire army to war. This is why the Bible tells us to carefully consider what comes out of our mouths.

Death and life are in the power of the tongue, And those who love it will eat its fruit.

Proverbs 18:21

THE ENIGMA OF THE TONGUE

Indeed, the tongue is an extremely powerful part of our bodies. In spite of its small size entire families have been destroyed simply because someone yielded their tongue to anger. In fact, wars have been started because a political leader said the wrong thing at the wrong time to the wrong person

See how great a forest a little fire kindles! And the tongue is a fire, a world of iniquity. The tongue is so set among our members that it defiles the whole body, and sets on fire the course of nature; and it is set on fire by hell. For every kind of beast and bird, of reptile and creature of the sea, is tamed and has been tamed by mankind. But no man can tame the tongue. It is an unruly evil, full of deadly poison. With it we bless our God and Father, and with it we curse men, who have been made in the similitude of God. Out of the same mouth proceed blessing and cursing. My brethren, these things ought not to be so.

Does a spring send forth fresh water and bitter from the same opening? Can a fig tree, my brethren, bear olives, or a grapevine bear figs? Thus no spring yields both salt water and fresh.

5. James 3:5b-12

There are several important lessons we must learn from this passage:

1. Just like a small spark can result in a catastrophic forest fire, a misspoken word can cause enormous damage.

2. If we want to consistently "eat the fruit" of God's promises, our lives must line up with God's Word and will. For this to happen, the words of our mouths need to be in harmony with His.

WHAT'S IN YOUR HEART?

We've already learned from the above passage in James that the tongue cannot be tamed. So, what can we possibly do, to keep us from aborting the faith process? I'm so glad you asked!

Everyone involved with computers knows the familiar phrase: garbage in, garbage out. What it basically means is that any data, information, or virus that enters a computer, whether intentionally or unintentionally, will eventually come out. The same applies to our hearts. The most secure way for us to prevent negative words from coming out of our mouths is to keep negative thoughts from penetrating our hearts.

"For out of the abundance of the heart the mouth speaks. A good man out of the good treasure of his heart brings forth good things, and an evil man out of the evil treasure brings forth evil things."

Matthew 12:34c, 35

BE CAREFUL WHAT YOU FILL YOUR "TANK" WITH

Allow me to share a story that might make you smile, but wasn't so funny when it happened:

In the early days of our ministry in Europe we'd purchased an old car that used gasoline instead of diesel, contrary to most automobiles there, which run on diesel fuel. Not being an expert on the subject I made the mistake of filling my tank with diesel. By the time I realized my mistake the car's tank was almost completely full. One well-meaning customer suggested that I fill the rest of the tank with gasoline. While I proceeded with the operation, I heard the man say, "Don't be surprised if it smokes a little at first."

"A little smoke" could not begin to describe the enormous cloud of smoke that came out of the tailpipe! We must have killed every insect within a mile radius! The car eventually stalled within a few hundred feet from the station and the tank had to be drained and then re-filled with fresh gasoline.

What I learned that day is that it matters what you fill your tank with. I'm also learning that it matters what we fill our hearts with because it will ultimately determine our Christian performance.

Finally, brethren, whatever things are true, whatever things are noble, whatever things are just, whatever things are pure, whatever things are lovely, whatever things are of good report, if there is any virtue and if there is anything praiseworthy — meditate on these things.

Philippians 4:8

To further emphasize the importance of setting our words in harmony with God's instructions, we can look at an event that took place right before the earthly birth of Jesus:

And the angel answered and said to him, "I am Gabriel, who stands in the presence of God, and was sent to speak to you and bring you these glad tidings. But behold, you will be mute and not able to speak until the day these things take place, because you did not believe my words which will be fulfilled in their own time."

Luke 1:19, 20

Because this had to do with a prophecy that had been announced many years before, Zacharias' confession did not prevent it from happening. However, his unbelieving words had dire consequences.

By the time his son was born, Zacharias had apparently learned his lesson. When he was asked what the name of his son should be, still not able to speak, he wrote on a tablet:

"His name is John." So they all marveled. Immediately his mouth was opened and his tongue loosed, and he spoke, praising God.

Luke 1:63, 64

WORDS CAN BE LETHAL

I'm sure we've all said things at one time or another that we wish we hadn't said. Fortunately, we can repent and ask for forgiveness when the opportunity presents itself.

Words carelessly uttered and not repented for will surely have dire consequences. We've already seen that Zachariah became mute as a result of his utterance. Let us look at another instance where misspoken words brought an even more disastrous outcome:

So an officer on whose hand the king leaned answered the man of God and said, "Look, if the LORD would make windows in heaven, could this thing be?" And he said, "In fact, you shall see it with your eyes, but you shall not eat of it."

2 Kings 7:2

I do not want to excuse this officer "on whose hand the king leaned," but I do want to describe the situation in which he found himself:

- So severe was the famine in the land that two mothers agreed to eat their own offspring.

- The king himself was despondent and had no solution to offer.

- The king was convinced the famine was of the Lord's doing.

- Based on the circumstance, the Word of God delivered by Elisha seems totally impossible.

- I have gone through a few difficult situations in my days, but nothing as severe as what the residents of this city went through! We would do well to remember this story next time we face adversity.

- To me, the king's inability to address the women's dilemma illustrates the futility of turning to the government for assistance. But don't get me started on politics!

- The situation is further complicated by the king's perception that the calamity came from the Lord. What we need to settle once and for all is that the Lord is not confused, nor is the Kingdom of God divided. The devil is the one who steals, kills, and destroys; not God!

- What these people were going through was catastrophic, and there was no solution in sight . . . humanly speaking.

- It is in such desperate situations that God's grace can shine, and when His glory can manifest in an awesome way. One of Paul's defining moments came when he heard the Lord building him up through the words: "My strength is made perfect in weakness." He expressed his clear understanding in his response, "For when I am weak, then I am strong."

"My grace is sufficient for you, for My strength is made perfect in weakness." Therefore most gladly I will rather boast in my infirmities, that the power of Christ may rest upon me. Therefore I take pleasure in infirmities, in reproaches, in needs, in persecutions, in distresses, for Christ's sake. For when I am weak, then I am strong.

2 Corinthians 12:9, 10

God spoke through Elisha in the midst of an impossible situation.

Just because some things are humanly impossible does not mean they're impossible for God. In fact, the more challenging the situation, the greater the opportunity for God to perform a miracle for which no man can possibly take the glory.

"The things which are impossible with men are possible with God."

Luke 18:27

The problem the officer in our story had was that he only considered human solutions in solving the desperate situation they were in. I'm sure not everyone is going to agree on what I'm about to say, but I believe that we should have a balanced approach when it comes to faith. I don't think we should systematically exclude the possibility of human intervention whenever we face a difficulty. If we suffer an illness, getting medical care through a physician may very well be the way God chooses to provide healing. The officer offended God by challenging the words of the prophet. He ended up seeing the miracle with his natural eyes, but did not partake of it.

As James taught us in the third chapter and fourth verse of his Epistle, our tongue serves pretty much like a rudder on a ship. Whether we realize or not, what comes out of our mouths determines the direction of our lives.

IF GOD BE FOR YOU . . .

One of my favorite stories in the Bible is found in the sixth chapter of 2 Kings:

Here we find Elisha and his servant surrounded by an army. Elisha's servant expressed the severity of the situation by saying, "Alas, my master! What shall we do?"

Evidently, nothing could have been done in the natural to save the day. However, Elisha wasn't relying on his natural eyesight. He had already seen the host of angels the Lord had provided. So he prayed that his servant's eyes of faith would be opened.

Then the LORD opened the eyes of the young man, and he saw. And behold, the mountain was full of horses and chariots of fire all around Elisha."

2 Kings 6:17b

CHAPTER 6

THE POWER OF PRAYER

It is impossible to talk about faith without making the connection to prayer.

While I enjoy immediate results as much as the next guy, I also realize that some answers do not come instantly. The very disciples Jesus had were empowered to cast out demons, but in at least one instance, were incapable to do so:

"this kind does not go out except by prayer and fasting ."

Matthew 17:21

This is a classic case of a group of people finding themselves up the creek without a proverbial paddle. How often have you found yourself in a similar situation? You made sure you had a word from the Lord on a particular subject, you crossed your spiritual T's and dotted every I, and yet, nothing seems to be happening.

Imagine how Daniel must have felt, as nothing in his situation seemed to be changing for three weeks! Thank God he continued to pray while God was at work behind the scenes.

Consider Elijah's dilemma as God asked him to pray for rain. His armor bearers continued to return with negative reports. But, praise the Lord, Elisha wasn't about to give up on what he'd already seen by the Spirit!

THE PRAYER OF FAITH

We must make a clear distinction between the prayer of faith and other kinds of prayers. Honestly, there are prayers that are more declarations of unbelief than actual prayers to God.

And the prayer of faith will save the sick, and the Lord will raise him up.

James 5:15a

Because the prayer of faith is based on spiritual fact rather than wishful aspirations, there are certain unmistakable characteristics about it. Allow me to point them out.

Some of these characteristics can be found in the very next verse:

The effective, fervent prayer of a righteous man avails much.

James 5:16b

The prayer of faith is **effective**. The reason for its effectiveness is that it is directed to God. It is not the vain recitation of a shopping list, or the registration of a complaint. The prayer of faith is focused on a clear objective, and it doesn't quit until that objective is reached.

It should be an encouragement to us to discover that Elijah was not a spiritual "giant," but "was" *a man with a nature like ours, but he prayed earnestly that it would not rain; and it did not rain on the land for three years and six months* (James 5:17).

The prayer of faith is **fervent**. Fervor isn't necessarily loud or boisterous. We shouldn't confuse exhibitionism, or one's attempt to draw attention to self for fervor. Like me, you've probably had to endure someone's long theatrical tirade, wondering if they were ever going to bring their so-called prayer to a close.

We really don't have to sound like Shakespeare to get God's attention. But we do have to be determined and passionate about the things we want God to do for us.

RECEIVE <u>WHEN</u> YOU PRAY

Faith is a now event. The answer we expect isn't something we're hoping to have happen in the future.

"Therefore I say to you, whatever things you ask when you pray, believe that you receive them, and you will have them."

Mark 11:24

Notice that Jesus didn't say, "If you pray," but rather, "when you pray." This tells us that prayer, just like faith, shouldn't be an occasional exercise or a last ditch effort when all else has failed. We shouldn't be like this lady whose husband had just been admitted to the hospital. When the doctor came to her after examining him and suggested they pray, her response was, "Is it so bad it has come to that?"

Back to our verse in the Gospel of Mark. Jesus tells us that when we pray we should receive whatever we've asked for right there and then. Why is that so important? Because if what we're asking for isn't available when we pray there is little chance that it ever will be!

It is surprising how open-minded we can be when it comes to earthly matters, while remaining skeptical in spiritual things. If the Internal Revenue Service was to send me a notice informing me that a tax refund has been deposited in my bank account, I would not hesitate to say that I have received my tax refund. Even though not a single penny has been withdrawn from the refund, there's no question that I have received it. Isn't it amazing that we seem to trust the IRS's word more than God's?

THE BETTER YOU KNOW HIM, THE MORE YOU WILL TRUST HIM

Have you ever felt like your prayers are bouncing right off the ceiling? Believe me, you're not alone! The reason this happens isn't that God is ignoring you, or that He has more important things to do. Just as your cell phone will not operate correctly if you're too far from a tower, it might be that you've allowed some distance between you and God. If you seem to be getting a "no service" signal when you pray, endeavor to get closer to Him and He will draw closer to you!

"If you abide in Me, and My words abide in you, you will ask what you desire, and it shall be done for you."

John 15:7

This brings us to the next point concerning faith and prayer: the trust issue. We have already touched on the subject in a previous chapter, but I want to bring out a point that is essential if we want to succeed in the faith process.

When Jesus talks about abiding in Him, it has great significance. There can be nothing casual about our relationship with the Lord. Abiding implies a close and intimate walk with Him. In the original Greek it implies taking-up residence with, or moving-in with. Many Christians are frustrated because they never seem to attain the level of intimacy they feel they should have with the Lord. If this fits you, please don't be offended by what I'm going to say, but this goal will continue to elude you if you insist on pursuing your own ways and holding on to sinful practices. Jesus will indeed open the door for you if you knock, but He simply won't let you bring in your old, dirty, rickety furniture!

The Apostle Paul taught us that there's a direct correlation between the degree that we know Jesus and how much of His resurrection power we will enjoy:

that I may know Him and the power of His resurrection,

Philippians 3:10a

Whenever we pray, our two primary objectives should be:

1. Know Jesus more intimately than we did before.

2. Lay at His feet anything that could possibly keep us from getting closer to Him.

PLEASE LET HIM TALK!

While we're on the subject of prayer, let me say that in its simplest expression, prayer is spending time in the presence of God.

We often think that prayer is a one way proposition with us doing all the talking! I've been married to my wife Josette for over 46 years. We've been together for so long we often finish each other's sentences. We know each other so well we don't have to say a word to communicate.

Be still , and know that I am God;

Psalm 46:10a

My mother always taught me that I shouldn't trust strangers. Our trust level will not go beyond the measure that we know Him. And the only way we can know Him is through the intimate relationship we acquire in prayer.

FOCUSED PRAYER

The first thing we need to address when it comes to prayer is to remember who it is that we're addressing our prayers to.

Some prayers sound more like a child's note to Santa Claus than actual prayers! Too often, like the woman at the well, we fail to recognize who it is we're talking to.

"If you knew the gift of God, and who it is who says to you, 'Give Me a drink,' you would have asked Him, and He would have given you living water."

John 4:10

In Psalm 69:13 David says it this way: "But as for me, my prayer is to You." Just as any important letter you're sending out, you absolutely make sure it is addressed to the right person.

Then we need to consider the rank and ability of Him who receives our petition. Remember that He is the all powerful Creator of the universe and nothing is impossible for Him.

Finally, our prayer has to be as focused and as precise as possible. There is a story in the Bible that perfectly illustrates that point. Here we find Elisha attempting to teach the King of Israel the very basics of prayer:

And he said, "Open the east window"; and he opened it. Then Elisha said, "Shoot"; and he shot. And he said, "The arrow of the LORD's deliverance and the arrow of deliverance from Syria; for you must strike the Syrians at Aphek till you have destroyed them." Then he said, "Take the arrows "; so he took them. And he said to the king of Israel, "Strike the ground"; so he struck three times, and stopped. And the man of God was angry with him, and said, "You should have struck five or six times; then you would have struck Syria till you had destroyed it! But now you will strike Syria only three times.

2 Kings 13:17-19

What lesson can we learn from this teaching session?

1. Elisha instructs the king to open a window, but just not any window. What's the significance of the east window? I don't know for sure, but what I do know is that we'd better follow to the letter any instructions the Lord gives us. Remember how Naaman had to dip in the river Jordan seven times? His healing totally depended on his obeying the instructions he'd received.

2. The king followed Elisha's instructions explicitly and totally depended on him to hear from God. He apparently had no ability to hear from God for himself.

3. Without Elisha's step by step "coaching," the king is totally helpless. Words to the wise: do not depend on someone else's relationship with God, or their ability to hear from him!

In all honesty, most of our prayers are helplessly selfish. More often than not, we pray for our family, our health, our finances, etc. It doesn't sound much like "seeking the Kingdom of God and His righteousness first" (Matthew 6:33) does it?

When it comes to prayer, the motivation of our heart is extremely important. Obviously, God will not grant you a request that has the sole purpose of gratifying the very flesh He wants us to crucify!

There are many plans in a man's heart, Nevertheless the LORD's counsel — that will stand.

Proverbs 19:21

When it's all said and done, God will only answer prayers that are offered in accordance to His will. This is why it's so important to know His perfect will and His will is found in His Word:

I beseech you therefore, brethren, by the mercies of God, that you present your bodies a living sacrifice, holy, acceptable to God, which is your reasonable service. And do not be conformed to this world, but be transformed by the renewing of your mind, that you may prove what is that good and acceptable and perfect will of God.

Romans 12:1, 2

CHAPTER 7

RIGHTLY POSITIONED FOR A MIRACLE

In the introduction of this book, I made you a simple promise: "You will not be confused by this book," and I intend to keep it.

All four Gospels contain numerous references to faith. Sometimes, Jesus wondered about the lack of faith of His disciples. Once, He even wondered where their faith was! But on at least two occasions, He went out of His way to point out the greatness of someone's faith.

I think we should pay particular attention to what made these two people special and maybe follow their example of faith:

And behold, a woman of Canaan came from that region and cried out to Him, saying, "Have mercy on me, O Lord, Son of David! My daughter is severely demon-possessed." But He answered her not a word. And His disciples came and urged Him, saying, "Send her away, for she cries out after us." But He answered and said, "I was not sent except to the lost sheep of the house of Israel." Then she came and worshiped Him, saying, "Lord, help me!" But He answered and said, "It is not good to take the children's bread and throw it to the little dogs." And she said, "Yes, Lord, yet even the little dogs eat the crumbs which fall from their masters' table." Then Jesus answered and said to her, "O woman, great is your faith! Let it be to you as you desire." And her daughter was healed from that very hour.

Matthew 15:22-28

Let us follow this Canaanite woman on her journey to her miracle:

1. She was perfectly conscious of her identity, not being an Israelite; thus, being disqualified to receive Jesus' attention.

2. If any doubts remained in her mind, they were completely dissipated by the disciples' counter recommendation. However, that didn't stop her from pursuing her miracle.

3. As if that wasn't enough, Jesus Himself turned her down! But did she give up? No, not on your life!

4. Talk about someone that was not easily offended. Not only was Jesus not giving her the time of day, but he actually called her a dog! But, it takes a lot more than an insult to deter someone as determined as she was!

5. What negotiating skills she possessed! How can anyone resist this kind of persistence? She was not contradicting what Jesus was saying. She was just pointing out the obvious: "even the little dogs eat the crumbs which fall from their masters' table."

It is because Jesus recognized that great determination and tenaciousness which characterized her exceptional faith, that Jesus told her, "great is your faith!"

You may want to think about that the next time you feel like giving up on your miracle just because it didn't come fast enough!

The other person Jesus points out as an example of noteworthy faith, is the Centurion.

Now when Jesus had entered Capernaum, a centurion came to Him, pleading with Him, saying, "Lord, my servant is lying at home paralyzed, dreadfully tormented." And Jesus said to him, "I will come and heal him." The centurion answered and said, "Lord, I am not worthy that You should come under my roof. But only speak a word, and my servant will be healed. For I also am a man under authority, having soldiers under me. And I say to this one, 'Go,' and he goes; and to another, 'Come,' and he comes; and to my servant, 'Do this,' and he does it." When Jesus heard it, He marveled, and said to those who followed, "Assuredly, I say to you, I have not found such great faith, not even in Israel!"

Matthew 8:5-10

1.   The first thing we need to point out is that the Centurion wasn't asking Jesus for anything for himself. His concern was for one of his servants.

2.   After Jesus agreed to go heal the man, the Centurion demonstrated a genuine sense of humility by declaring his unworthiness in having Jesus come to his house.

3. Next, the centurion expressed his deep understanding of the faith process: if he can only hear Jesus pronounce a word of healing, then nothing more is necessary.

4. Finally, we discover how the recognition of authority is essential to the faith process. The Centurion knew that once the command of healing had been issued by Jesus, the deliverance of his servant would be the only possible outcome.

5. No matter who we are or how unworthy we may feel, we're capable of great faith, that even Jesus will marvel at!

LET GOD BE GOD!

In the chapter dedicated to prayer we explained how important it is to recognize who it is that we're addressing our prayers to. God is not a facilitator and even less Santa Claus!

To illustrate the importance of properly identifying the Author of our faith, there's one story in the Bible that stands out:

Now a certain man was there who had an infirmity thirty-eight years. When Jesus saw him lying there, and knew that he already had been in that condition a long time, He said to him, "Do you want to be made well?" The sick man answered Him, "Sir, I have no man to put me into the pool when the water is stirred up; but while I am coming, another steps down before me."Jesus said to him, "Rise, take up your bed and walk." And immediately the man was made well, took up his bed, and walked.

John 5:5-9

There's no doubt this man wanted to be healed of his infirmity. Why else would he come to the pool of Bethesda day after day hoping to get the miracle he had been waiting 38 years for?

When Jesus asked him the question, "Do you want to be made well," why wasn't he quick to answer, "Yes, I do"? Apparently, he mistakenly identified Jesus as a possible candidate to carry him into the water.

He failed to realize that the One asking him the question had the power to change his life forever!

If we are to receive from God all that He promises in His Word it is essential that we give Him the liberty to provide the object of our request when and how He wants to provide it. Naaman, who desperately needed a healing from leprosy, almost didn't receive it because he insisted on having it his way.

If your attitude is "It's my way, or the highway," it may work with some people some of the time, but it certainly won't work with God. You may be a fan of old "Ol' Blue Eyes," but you really don't want to be singing "I did it my way" in the presence of Almighty God.

POSITIONED TO RECEIVE

What I'm about to say is in direct contradiction with what is taught in many modern churches today. As much as God loves us and wants to give us all that pertains to life and godliness, receiving His grace in a particular area is not unconditional, but contingent upon several factors:

1. The first condition is faith on the part of the one that is to receive (Ephesians 2:8).

2. The second is that the relationship between He that gives and the one who receives is not interrupted by unforgiven sin.

3. The third has to do with obedience. If we are to receive from God, we need to be where He wants us to be both spiritually and physically.

Allow me to elaborate on this third condition. Naaman had to dip in the river Jordan to receive his healing and not in any other river, no matter how great. If Elijah was to enjoy the supernatural provision of the Lord during the famine, he had to be at Cherith and not a place of his choosing. Jonah had to be in Nineveh to be used by God in the deliverance of the city.

Take it from someone who had to learn this lesson the hard way: you can only enjoy the peace, joy, and blessings of the Lord if you are where He has asked you to be.

Before I even learned what a prophetic word was, one was given to me by the pastor of the first church my family ever attended. I don't remember most of it, but the most important part was this, "You will minister My Word to your own people".

"This could not possibly be the Lord speaking to me," I thought. I quickly dismissed it for what I thought to be two valid reasons. Reason one, I had just been freshly saved and had no ministerial skills. Second, ministering to my own people meant going back to France. In my lightning fast mind I figured this wasn't going to happen. After all, my wife and I had immigrated from there with no intention to ever move back.

Since my assignment was supposedly east of where we were living, I thought the best thing I could do, while I was at an age that still qualified, was to heed the words of the song, "Go west, young man" and move my family to Colorado.

The following 12 years were some of the worst years of my entire life. Not only was I miserable, but I seemed to make everyone around me miserable as well. Those years in the proverbial "wilderness" taught me the importance of being in God's perfect will and being at the exact location He has chosen for you. Jonah and I found out that even though God continues to love us and His mercies are still extended to us, we're simply out of position to benefit from His abundant grace.

When we fail to obey Him and go where we choose to go and do what we choose to do, we're like the football receiver that was signaled to move to a certain spot on the field, but for some reason, failed to do so. What could have been the winning touchdown reception ends up being an incomplete pass, or even worse, a disastrous interception!

I will never forget the wonderful way the Lord finally brought me out of my disobedience. I distinctly remember being presented with what appeared to be a legal document. What was special about this "contract" is that nothing was written on this blank page except for a date in the upper left corner and the instruction, "Your signature here," in the lower right corner of the same page. I tried to argue with the fact that there were no paragraphs on this document, and that I was not in the habit of signing what seemed to be the equivalent of a blank check. This

is when the Lord asked me a very close and personal question: "You've been writing every paragraph of your life for the past 12 years, how do you like it?"

Without bothering to answer, I promptly "signed" the aforementioned "document." Even since that all important day, I've been watching God do the most wonderful things in and through my life!

THE NARROW ROAD

The most popular teaching of the day sounds very much like a commercial for a fast food restaurant: "Have it your way." This may not be a bad thing if all you're doing is ordering a custom built hamburger. But when it comes to receiving from God, you better follow the protocol He has so clearly established in His Word. There is a way to approach Him, as well as a heart attitude to emulate, before we can partake of His grace.

"Enter by the narrow gate; for wide is the gate and broad is the way that leads to destruction, and there are many who go in by it. Because narrow is the gate and difficult is the way which leads to life, and there are few who find it."

Matthew 7:13, 14

This doesn't sound like we can come to God any way we want and He'll just have to grant us whatever we ask Him for, does it?

Modern grace teachers would have us believe that no matter how unrighteous our behavior might be, there's nothing that can keep us from receiving from God.

While it's true nothing can separate us from God's love and our salvation is not contingent on how good or bad we have been, there cannot be any sin we've not repented of standing between us and our merciful God who's ready to forgive us.

The belief that God has changed His spiritual laws in order to accommodate modern rebellious, sinful men and women is as crazy as believing that the law of gravity is no longer in effect. If someone wants to prove me wrong on this point, they are welcome to jump out of an airplane without a parachute, or refuse to repent of a known sin and have God spontaneously grant their request.

I realize what I'm telling you may sound difficult. I'm also aware what I'm teaching here goes counter current to what is being taught in many pulpits today. If you're having trouble accepting this, remember the words of Jesus in the passage we just read: *"for wide is the gate and broad is the way that leads to destruction, and there are many who go in by it. Because narrow is the gate and difficult is the way which leads to life, and there are few who find it."*

Also, remember that the direction taken by the majority is rarely the correct one. The majority of the people who had followed Jesus during his three and a half years of ministry are the very people who asked for Jesus to be crucified!

DON'T STAY IN THE BOAT

Hear my heart when I say that the walk of faith is not for the fainthearted, or for anyone who consistently chooses the path of least resistance.

Obviously, Peter had much to learn when it came to faith, but we should at least admire his courage when he stepped out of the boat after Jesus ordered him to join Him on the waves.

I'm sure the other disciples must have wondered what had come over their friend when he made his request. Why would you want to leave the safety of a perfectly good boat to brave a stormy sea? I also suppose that their wondering turned to envy when they saw Peter actually walking on the water.

If indeed you have heard the voice of Jesus telling you to "Come," don't let your fear of the unknown, or doubts about your own abilities keep you from stepping out in faith.

For the sake of illustration, let me share the testimony of a miracle that occurred during one of our mission trips to Cote d'Ivoire, Africa. We had clearly heard God's voice concerning a medical mission at the prison of Bouake. We firmly believed what has become somewhat of a cliché: "When God gives a vision, He makes provision."

We arrived in Abidjan with the assurance that our mission would be completed. When we approached the Ivorian customs, however, we were told that the medical supplies we had shipped via air cargo would not be released until several days past our date of departure. As we gathered our team in prayer, God clearly told us to proceed with the mission with or without the supplies.

Since we had very limited financial resources, we stopped at a local pharmacy to purchase just enough medication to treat about 30 patients. The problem was the prison had over 2,000 inmates with 95% of them suffering from some form of illness!

For those of you who are new to the faith adventure, what I'm about to share with you might be hard to believe, but it's absolutely true. We began our medical clinic as scheduled with whatever supplies we had on hand. My wife, Josette, was in charge of dispensing the medication Dr. Clementine was prescribing for each patient. As the day progressed, our doctor began to wonder how there could possibly be any medication

Left; especially the antibiotic treatments she had prescribed extensively. When she attempted to check on the status, my wife asked her not to worry and just keep on writing prescriptions. By then, my wife had already been made aware of a miracle in progress.

At end of three days of our medial clinic, several hundred prisoners had received full treatments; and we still had medication leftover!

Had we been looking for a miracle? Certainly not before our medical supplies became held-up in customs. But God, Who wanted these prisoners healed even more than we did, multiplied the medication and received all the glory for doing it!

AS LONG AS THERE'S ONE...

I believe it is God's will for us to use our faith and seek a supernatural solution to every problem we face. But, just as Jesus involved His disciples in the multiplication of food miracles, God looks for a man or woman of faith to work through.

He saw that there was no man, And wondered that there was no intercessor; Therefore His own arm brought salvation for Him; And His own righteousness, it sustained Him.

Isaiah 59:16

I will never forget the day God raised a man from the dead during one of our missions to the Bouake prison.

We had just completed yet another medical intervention at the prison facility where working conditions were less than desirable to say the least! My wife and I were looking forward to cleaning up and resting after a horrendous day in 110° temperatures.

As we were preparing to exit the prison, our friend, whom we called, "Major," and who was in charge of medical care at the facility, intercepted us and asked us to pray for a man he described as a "Very sick prisoner." My wife and I entered the building where we found the "sick man" lying on the floor. We began to pray for him, but then discovered that his body was unusually cold for being in such a hot environment. Having had previous medical training, my wife began to check the man's pulse, but found none!

You might have commanded the man to, "Rise up, in the name of Jesus!" But we didn't. We left the facility thinking we had been called in too late to pray for his healing.

When we returned to the prison the next day, "Major" came running out of his office to meet us. "Do you know what happened to the man you prayed for yesterday?" Before we could provide him with an answer he announced that several hours after our departure the man had suddenly sat up, looked around, asked how he had gotten there, and immediately asked for some food. He ultimately stood up and walked back to his quarters under his own power!

I've been asked many times why there are so many more instances of miraculous healings in third world countries than there seem to be in more affluent societies. The answer is simple: when someone in Europe or North America needs medical help, he can usually get it by calling a doctor or by going to the emergency room. If someone gets ill in a remote African village, a telephone may not be readily available, and transportation to a medical facility may be an issue.

Does this mean believers in developed countries need less faith than those living in Africa? Not at all! It's just that the former have more opportunity to practice their faith than those who ignorantly think they don't need to.

YOU'RE QUALIFIED

The last thing I want to say on being rightly positioned for a miracle is that you don't have to be perfect, nor do you have to be a spiritually mature Christian to experience the grace of God through faith.

To prove this point, allow me to share an experience my wife and I had in the early days of our Christian journey.

At the time, we belonged to a church that was birthed during the Jesus Movement. A number of ex-drug addicts and former hippies lived in the basement of the church and were being mentored by the Pastor.

Whether intentionally or not, the Pastor would routinely come visit us precisely at dinner time. He would show up with a van filled with five or six of his young "disciples." Since the visit was totally unexpected, my wife had barely enough food prepared to feed our small family of three. But, she simply didn't have the heart to send our wonderful brothers away with empty stomachs.

The following occurred on several occasions. No matter what would be on the evening's menu, adequate portions of meat and fixings would be served to everyone, but whatever remained in the pot never seemed to diminish, even when several of the guests would request seconds!

My point in sharing this testimony, is to encourage you in the development of your faith, no matter where you may be in your Christian walk.

WHO IS JUST?

Since spiritual maturity and great Bible knowledge aren't required for us to enjoy the benefits of faith, what criteria, if any, are we supposed to meet to spiritually qualify?

For I am not ashamed of the gospel of Christ, for it is the power of God to salvation for everyone who believes, for the Jew first and also for the Greek. For in it the righteousness of God is revealed from faith to faith; as it is written, "The just shall live by faith."

Romans 1:16, 17

We understand from this passage of Scripture that national identity, or anything else for that matter, cannot disqualify anyone from receiving the power of God.

There are two key words in this verse that we need to give close attention to: **righteousness** and **just**. Since none of us are righteous, not one (Romans 3:10), we understand that if any righteousness is to be found, it will be in God and from God. However, when it comes to being just, that is completely up to us.

I have hope in God, which they themselves also accept, that there will be a resurrection of the dead, both of the just and the unjust . This being so, I myself always strive to have a conscience without offense toward God and men.

Acts 24:15, 16

While there is absolutely nothing we can do to be found righteous, except to receive the righteousness of God through the redemptive work of Jesus, it is our absolute responsibility to maintain "a conscience without offense toward God and men"!

If there is anything in our lives that we know to be an offense to Our God, we must be quick to repent of it. Failure to do so will make us "unjust," and therefore, unqualified to live by faith.

Let us not be deceived by those who try to teach repentance is obsolete. Remember that Jesus is faithful and just to forgive us our sins and to cleanse us from all unrighteousness (1 John 1:9).

CONCLUSION

I pray that now that you've finished reading this book you are better equipped than ever to embark on the wonderful journey of faith.

You are about to discover the fullness of what God has wanted you to enjoy all along. He has prepared things for you the natural mind cannot conceive, and the natural eye cannot behold.

I'm sure we've all dreamt about going on a search for a hidden treasure. The amazing blessings God has in store for you that you're about to discover are infinitely more valuable than anything any rich pirate could have buried!

To be sure, the challenge given in Malachi 3:10 has to do with finances. But, I don't believe that it is limited to the realm of finances. Whether in the area of healing, emotional blessing, finances or personal fulfillment, I invite you to give faith a try. If moving a mole hill is a challenge for you, you may not want to tackle Mount Everest just yet. You can still start somewhere.

I can promise you this: as you build your confidence and become used to "climbing on God's back" in faith, walking by faith will eventually become second nature to you. Because it is the way God intended for us to proceed through life on this earth, you will experience the peace of God as you've never felt it before. And, because your life will conform more and more to the "roadmap" that represents your destiny, may you see God bearing witness both with signs and wonders, with various miracles, and gifts of the Holy Spirit, (Hebrews 2:4).

ENDORSEMENTS

"Faith That Actually Works" is one of the best books I have read on the subject of "Faith". I have been teaching faith to some degree for over 40 years and wish I had used this book as a guide. Of course I couldn't because it is just now being published. I believe everyone whether they are a new Christian or a Teacher, Pastor, Evangelist or a seasoned Christian, can grow in faith as they study this book. Rev. Jean Paul Engler has written this in a language so simple, yet deep, it has the power to reach all that will take the time to read and study it's content. The illustrations are excellent and clearly explain the point he is trying to make.

Pastor David Bentley

In Luke 18:18 Jesus makes it clear, He was concerned about whether He would find faith on the Earth when He returned. "Faith that Actually Works" by Jean Paul Engler, serves as a great handbook on understanding, exercising, and walking by faith. It is written in a way that both the new believer and the faith veteran will be nourished and strengthened by it's content. Hebrews 11 teaches us without faith it's impossible to please God... The principles in this book will help move you into the "God pleaser" category.

Pastor Jeff Hall
Community Faith Church, Holt, M

Jean-Paul Engler has written a timely, balanced, practical, Biblically based manual on faith. You will find out why faith is so important, where it comes from and how to use it, all in one concise book. For the uninformed, the misinformed and even the well informed, you are going to love this book. I know, I did.

Pastor Michael Williams
International Outreach Center

OTHER BOOKS

By Rev. Jean-Paul Engler

A NEW DAY FOR MISSIONS

A comprehensive booklet on modern missions, for both those who're preparing for missions work and those who are called to support it.

THE WINNING CHURCH

A book that describes where the Church stands today compared to how Jesus expects to find her when He returns. It also provides abundant scriptural instructions on how to be more effective as a member of the Body and preparing the Church for His imminent return.

GRACE ANATOMY

This book presents a balanced approach on the subject of grace and provides believers effective scriptural weapons to fight the negative effects of the hyper grace teachings.

THE UNHOLY ALLIANCE

In this book, Rev. Engler reveals the end-time strategy involving three evil spiritual entities bent on the destruction of Israel. America and the Church of Jesus-Christ

L'EGLISE QUI GAGNE

A French translation of the "Winning Church" book, by the same author.

All books listed above as well as additional copies of this book, can be ordered through Amazon.com or directly at

FSCO – PO Box 423 – NEW MARKET, TN – 37820

22791338R00052

Made in the USA
Middletown, DE
09 August 2015